To my two sons, Daniel and Cory
You inspire me to become more every day.

WHAT IS YOUR DESTINY?

Manifest More Health, Happiness, and Success

Wendi Blum

LIVE YOUR TRUTH PUBLISHING, INC.
Hutchinson Island, FL

The author of this book does not prescribe the use of any technique as a form of treatment for physical, emotional, or medical problems without the advice of a healthcare professional, either directly or indirectly. The intent of the author is only to offer information of a general nature to help you in your quest for emotional and spiritual well-being.

Published and distributed by
Success Blueprint
Boca Raton, FL
Website: www.wendiblum.com

Cover and interior design by The Book Couple

Printed in the United States of America

CONTENTS

APPENDICES

ACKNOWLEDGMENTS

To my two wonderful sons. You are the reason I decided to re-create my destiny. Thank you for being my wake-up call and teaching me life's most valuable lessons . . . unconditional love, unwavering faith, and the power of choice.

Dad, you have been my North Star. Your grace, gentleness, and smile continue to be my compass. Thank you for shining your bright light from up above.

To Aunt Mahsee and Uncle Teddy, thank you for being the wind beneath my wings. You gifted me the power of simplicity, authenticity, and connection.

To Mom, thank you for modeling how to never ever give up even when the tides get really high.

To Jeff Murray and Judy Katz. I had the great honor to work for you as you demonstrated what impeccable character and great leadership looked like. I watched and learned so much from each one of you.

To Dr. Chris Obrien. Thank you for believing in the power of this work and trusting me with your difficult cases.

To Nina, my friend and very first client, thank you for doing the work and then showing me what was possible. I know you are sparkling your magic from the heavens above.

To Mary Ann Morgan Fried. You appeared like a beautiful butterfly, and I am most blessed to have you in my life.

To Leslie Glickman, you have been my incredible yoga mentor, dear friend, retreat partner, and so much more. I am so grateful for you and the entire Yoga Journey Studio community for being my safe harbor and my home.

To Paul, I overflow with appreciation for your open, loving, and giving heart. You have added so much dimension, so much richness, happiness, and love into my life. Thank you for your willingness to bring a whole new layer of spiritual ritual into both of our lives.

A big heartfelt sprinkle of gratitude to my inspirational teachers who have led the way: Marianne Williamson, Michael Beckwith, Sonia Choquette, Michelle Bernstein, and Louise Hay. A big shout out of appreciation to Suzanne Evans and David Neagle for being the real deal and helping me break through the terror barrier so that I could share this work.

To all of the beautiful souls who attended numerous workshops, retreats, and privately coached with me. Each one of you left a soul print on my heart. You inspired me to keep doing this work even when my own challenges came up.

To those who the Universe put in my path to help me write this book. I am incredibly humbled and grateful. Thank you, Carol and Gary, for saying yes to this woman with a big vision, dream, and short timeline. Thank you to Brittany for the many hours of proofreading and designing that went into this project. You always say yes, and I am so lucky to have you on my team. Much gratitude to Monica for her artistic flare, to Lamise for always having her camera beside her yoga mat, and for Jack Shulman for having his video camera ready to go. It takes a village, and I have been blessed to have a group of extraordinary and generous people in my life.

And lastly, I must thank my angels, guides, and God. I now know you are there watching over me. I feel your flow of love and divine presence every day. I send you Endless, Boundless, Limitless, Eternal Love and Gratitude.

PREFACE

Hello, beautiful, gifted, talented friend. I am bursting with happiness to share this book with you. If you can feel the vibe of my excitement in these words, it is because you and I are about to embark on a Destiny together. This journey is intended to take you to a life overflowing with smiles, laughter, abundance, and success. I am blissfully grateful that I discovered this path, and I want you join me. It sparkles with glistening bright light shining the way so that you can follow the illumination to discover your own divine destiny.

It was only seven years ago that I was surrounded by shadows of darkness.

I was forty-five years old, working a corporate job in the pharmaceutical industry, and from the outside, it looked like life was really good, but on the inside, I was feeling empty, lost, and blue. My life was passing me by, and I felt like an imposter. I was going through the motions of hanging out with friends, spending time with family, and working my career, but something felt off. Everything around me seemed so superficial—chatting on the cell phone for hours, shopping for new clothes I didn't need, spending hours on my hair and makeup. My secret self was hiding beneath my fears, anxieties, feelings of worthlessness, and despair. I didn't want to be judged, so I didn't tell anyone. I secretly buried my troubles in a couple glasses of red wine topped with a sugar fix every night. I would wake up feeling guilty and then go through another day exactly the same way. It was a vicious cycle that I just couldn't seem to break.

My awakening happened in two stages. The first wave of my awareness happened the night of the 9-11 tragedy. I was in an abusive relationship with a man I had been engaged to for eight years. I didn't think I could get out of it. I went to counseling for many years and still felt powerless and unable to leave. Then September 11th happened.

The day after that dark day, I somehow was able to tap into a power I did not know I had and made the break. I became empowered by asking questions I had never asked before: "Why them and not me?" I had been on the verge of suicide my whole life and felt I offered no value, so why would someone else be randomly chosen to die over me? I thought about how I lived every day in fear versus all the beautiful souls that on that one day just went to work without any fear and died.

How could that be? I had to honor them. I had to leave. I asked one last question that became my life's quest: "If today was your last day, Wendi, have you lived your greatest and highest purpose? What is your destiny?" And suddenly I became courageous enough to ask my ex-fiancé to leave. That was phase one: I asked new questions.

But as life went forward, I became weak again. Some areas in my life improved, while others spiraled downward. Until that night . . .

It was 1:00 in the morning, and I was having another anxiety attack. I couldn't breathe. I lay awake in bed and did a mathematical calculation. I was forty-five. The average life span of a women is eighty-eight years. I could potentially live another forty-three years. Yikes! That really scared me. I was in so much emotional pain that I couldn't bare the thought of living that long filled with that much fear. My insides hurt. I thought I would literally die of fear.

Then I somehow shifted for a micro-moment, and one single word popped into my awareness as if it had been downloaded from a divine source of possibility. That word was NO. I said it over and over again: "NO, NO, NO." I felt a spark of some sort of energy enter into my body. I didn't know how I would implement this new idea of "NO" into my life or what the YES would look like, but it really didn't matter. For the first time ever, I said NO to my fear. The next day my life changed.

I woke up and decided to do everything in reverse. I had been so incredibly busy. I was surrounded by lots of people. I was always doing something for someone else. I worked endless hours. I was a "doing machine." And I just stopped. That day, I started out on a new path, and this one included lots of questions starting with "Is there anyone anywhere who is living a life where they feel happy, whole, and free?" And although I couldn't think of anyone I knew directly, I had suspected there were, and I decided to go on a quest to find them. Then another brand-new thought popped into my awareness: perhaps I was in some way responsible for the outcome of the circumstances in my life. The idea startled me and even sounded crazy at first, but now I was open enough to play with the possibility that maybe it was true. Boy was my life getting ready to undergo an overhaul.

My first zone of change began where I was most comfortable: working out in the gym. I would binge eat and then head to the gym to work out for hours to burn off the load of calories. Sound familiar? It was one of my deep, dark secrets. So I bought some Sharpies and wrote a health and fitness affirmation on a T-shirt. I would say the mantra while working out. I would repeat, "My destiny is to eat healthy. My destiny is to exercise. My destiny is to achieve results. My destiny is to have a strong and healthy body."

The more I declared my desires, the more disciplined I became. The words vibrated something powerful, but I wasn't really aware at the time that I was actually reprogramming my brain and tapping into the Law of Attraction. I had no idea.

My creativity started to kick in. It was like I was picking up a new channel on the radio that I didn't even know existed, and I loved it. It was filled with inspiration, and it wanted to express itself through me. I couldn't stop writing affirmations for my T-shirts. . . .

My Destiny Is to Be Strong.
My Destiny Is to Be Powerful.
My Destiny Is to Be Courageous.
My Destiny Is to Be Fearless.

The messages and power statements were running through my mind 24-7. I became addicted to the way they made me feel. I was feeling invigorated, happy, and free, and I wanted to share that feeling with everyone.

Not only was I repeating these mantras, but I started to quiet my mind with meditation. Being an extremist, I would attempt hours of meditation at a time, and then one day it happened. My mind started to slow down. Then life got really interesting. All of these amazing things started to happen. I was feeling incredibly alive, and I was actually attracting goodness into my life . . . miracles were showing up *everywhere*.

What happened?

Somehow I knew that the coincidences that were occurring almost daily in my life were happening because of the inner work I was doing. The more I believed, the more they happened. And since I had a pharmaceutical background, I applied metrics to everything the way a clinical trial uses patterns and sequences. I was in awe. I had accidently discovered what the great thought leaders have known since the beginning of time: how to create miracles. So, you may ask . . .

Are they available to everyone? Is there a miracle on the verge of happening to you? Are there steps you can take to actually manifest more miracles into your life, right here, right now? If you would have asked me those questions ten years ago, I would have said yes, but it would have been a completely different kind of yes then I know to be true today (now with complete, unwavering, undeniable conviction and knowing).

I believe miracles are everywhere, and I think about them on a daily basis throughout the day. See, most people grow their awareness and desire around miracles when something difficult comes into their life. What if challenges are disguised miracles that are here to help you awaken? Perhaps you have a miracle beside you right now on the other side of your greatest setback. What if one small shift in your perception can open your heart and dial you into that vibration that will attract that miracle and many more?

If you are reading this now, your higher destiny is calling you.

So now you know, you get to decide:

What is your destiny?

INTRODUCTION

"What is your destiny?" is a powerful question that, once asked, will forever change your life. So now that you have decided you are ready for more health, happiness, and success in your life, how is this new journey going to unfold?

The purpose of this book is to help guide you along the mysterious path of life. My experience coaching hundreds of people has validated the power of the methods, processes, and techniques that I share with you in this book. I'm your partner, your teammate, and your guide throughout this process. My purpose and passion are to help you tap into your power, unleash your brilliance, and live a life you love—right now.

Through the "What Is Your Destiny?" process, you will discover the power that exists inside of you to do, have, or be anyone that you choose. In any moment, you get to decide . . . or even begin all over again. You can design your desired life, business, or future through the releasing process of letting go; then the focusing process of gaining clarity around your dreams, desires, and goals; and then the discipline process to plant seeds through visualization and inspired action. Your thoughts, feelings, and actions are that powerful. The chapters in this book outline different aspects of the self-discovery process and help you move into an expanded consciousness of awareness.

So let's say you want more happiness. First, identifying what you *don't* want helps you to realize with clarity what you *do* want. Then, you can start to consciously let go of the circumstance you no longer desire, thereby creating space for something better to come into your life.

Next, speaking the Destiny Power Statements out loud repetitively over a period of time activates the reprogramming process. By focusing your thoughts on the desired feelings and outcomes, new neural pathways are formed, and the brain is actually reshaped, bringing about desired changes in your day-to-day experiences. This step alone will bring about positive results in your life.

As more and more goodness comes into your life, your belief system will strengthen, bringing in even more faith—one of the key ingredients to creating a new, enhanced Destiny. A spark of divine creative flow will add yet another layer of charged energy that lights your way to a whole new life of possibility.

All of this is yours. You will be inspired to boldly move forward to take your life to the next level. You will courageously blast through obstacles regardless of the fear that in the past would have held you back.

The shirt I am wearing on the cover of this book has a picture of a yellow butterfly on it to symbolize the metamorphosis you are about to experience, just like a caterpillar who becomes a butterfly. One ending is just another beginning. You are about to set yourself free.

Each chapter starts with a Destiny Power Statement followed by a transformation. The mantra is to be repeated over and over again throughout the day. The more feeling you attach to each statement as you speak it, the more power is released into the energetic field around you. Your energy matches up with the same frequency at which you vibrate and attracts something similar back into your life. Life is a boomerang.

Once you add your big why, mission, vision, and passion into the equation, your vibration gets even stronger. Each step of the way, you will be adding another piece to the destiny puzzle.

The breath work and meditation described at the end of the book will add another dimension to further deepen the work. Using the power of visualization by actually imagining your desired outcome with great detail as if it has already happened imprints into the subconscious mind an intuitive knowing of how to create that outcome. Your brain does not know the difference between something imagined or real, so feel happy and grateful in advance. It is those feelings that send out the high vibration that magnetizes something similar or even better into your life.

This is just the beginning for you. Get ready to shine.

MIRACLES

My Destiny Is to Believe in Miracles
My Destiny Is to Create Miracles
My Destiny Is to Receive Miracles
My Destiny Is to Be a Miracle

One of the very first clients in my life coaching practice was referred to me from the hematology department at the University of Miami. He came to see me on the strong recommendation of his doctor since he was on the transplant list due to fatty liver, and he needed to lose weight pronto so that his medical condition wouldn't worsen.

His wife persuaded him to see me, and she agreed to accompany him for each one of our sessions since he was so reluctant. Four sessions later, after a series of exercises (some of which are included in this book) that consisted of writing, speaking, and listening to "Power Statements," breathing exercises, meditations, and future scripting, his liver disease reversed.

In an instant, I had a shift in perspective, and so did this client. If it can happen for one, then this same kind of miracle is available to everyone. The crazy-good part is that it can be something small like getting a good parking spot or something really big like recovering from a life-threatening disease.

What I know to be true is that in this very instant there is a miracle waiting to be discovered, willed, and activated inside of you (and, yes, you *are* that valuable and precious). Today, notice your first miracle by inhaling in this new day. Believe miracles are possible for you. Set an intention to manifest miracles in your life and acknowledge that just being alive means you already have created one.

PEACE

My Destiny Is to Be Peace
My Destiny Is to Be Calm
My Destiny Is to Be Centered
My Destiny Is to Be Balanced

In my past life, I was none of the above. I was completely overwhelmed, stressed out, and barely holding on. I was a mess. On the outside, I could put up a good front. I looked like I had my act together, but on the inside, I was tied in knots. As I mentioned in the preface, it wasn't until I did a mathematical equation at 1:00 in the morning that I realized I could not take it anymore. I would die of anxiety, worry, and sheer exhaustion. I had another forty-three years to reach the average life span of a woman these days, but I kept thinking, *I won't make it. I can't do this. Something has to change.* And then I said the one word that shifted into so much more over the coming years. I said, "NO more. NO, NO, and NO." I didn't know how I was going to change my life, but I finally said, "No more of this crap. No more of this pain. No more of this despair."

The next morning, I started a brand-new routine by asking one simple question. I already knew the long list of all of the things I had been doing all along, like driving the early morning carpool shift to school, working sixty hours a week, sports, laundry, dinner, etc., etc., but what hadn't I been doing? I certainly didn't relax because I had so much to do, and I most certainly didn't slow down because I thought I couldn't or my world would fall apart.

But one thought luckily dropped into my awareness. "What if I was wrong?"

I was jolted when I heard that message come from my inside, but it came again: "What if everything is reversed? What if you slow down and get still?"

So, out of desperation, I did, and my life forever changed. That quiet time became a meditation practice that shifted my perspective so profoundly that it brought abundant peace, tranquility, and happiness into my life. It infused my soul with freedom and so much more.

Now I would be remiss without sharing that developing a practice requires discipline, but if I can do it, so can you. Go slow and be patient. Just find a sacred space in your home and start by connecting with your breath. Focus on your inhale and notice how the breath brings about a sense of calm. Then on the exhale, just observe.

Now gently bring your awareness to the base of your spine and imagine a ruby-red light moving in a circular motion. Feel a connection to mother earth and the ground beneath you. Just observe without judgment. Now, imagine the color orange at the navel area. See a brilliant, bright orange light moving again in circular motion. Just observe.

Move that light upward a couple of inches and see the color yellow fill your entire core area. Breathe in the color of the sun. Then imagine your heart enveloped in an emerald green light, pulsating and vibrating all shades of green. Move that light up to the throat area and see the color blue, like the ocean running up and down your vocal cords. Just notice the variety of blue light filling up this space. Now move that light up to the area between your brow.

See a purple glow shining inward and projecting outward at the same time. Observe with the inner eye. Now, see the light spiral upward and shining brightly like diamonds in the sky at the crown of the head. All color and no color merging into the entire Universe. Allow that flow of energy to move back and forth, creating a peaceful sensation in your body.

Note: You can download one of my guided meditations at www.wendiblummeditations.com.

GRATEFUL

My Destiny Is to Be Grateful
My Destiny Is to Be Thankful
My Destiny Is to Be Appreciative
My Destiny Is to Count My Blessings

For the most part, children are trained to say, "Thank you" from a young age when they receive something, usually in the form of a gift or something else in material form. I used the phrases "please" and "thank you" myself, but they were merely words until I discovered a much deeper level of the power of gratitude. Many times, words are merely conditioned into the subconscious mind through repetition and therefore become automatic in one's language. Speaking something and really feeling it aren't always totally synchronized. There is a big difference, and it really does matter. What one speaks is important; what ones says and feels is where the real power is. The "say it, mean it, feel it" vibration is the one that has the magnetizing zest in it.

Because I had felt so lonely, depressed, and victimized for so many years, and those feelings were dissipating, I started to feel gratitude at a much higher level than I had ever experienced before. Tears of appreciation would roll down my cheeks almost daily (and still do) because I would feel so lucky. You know that feeling when you are looking for your keys and you find them in your purse or pocket of your jeans, realizing they were there the whole time. I was looking for the keys to a vehicle that would drive me home to a happy, fulfilled life, and I found them in my own pocket. I became beyond grateful, which is why I decided to dedicate my life in gratitude and give this information back to those who are seeking more goodness and happiness in their lives, too.

Gratitude all by itself will bring more to be grateful for into your life. I ask my clients to rate their level of happiness on a scale of 1 to 10 (with 10 being the happiest), and then I ask them to write a list of ten things they are grateful for every day for seven days. One week later, I ask them that same question and their rating level on the happiness scale always goes up a few notches.

If you feel blue, make your list too. It sounds simple, yet it creates a shift in perspective that echoes more of the same vibe right back to you.

Gratitude brings about a good attitude.

BODY

My Destiny Is to Love My Body
My Destiny Is to Be Fit
My Destiny Is to Be Toned
My Destiny Is to Have
a Strong and Healthy Body

The physical body you currently have is the one possession that will remain yours throughout your entire lifetime no matter what. It's yours. You can't trade it in. You can love other people, your home, your car, and even your pet, but the love and care for your physical body matters most. Your body houses your mind, your heart, and your life.

This is the one area I thought I had covered. For the most part, I worked out several days a week and ate what I thought was mostly healthy. It wasn't until I realized I was living a lie that I could break through the barriers of denial. I wanted to have my cake and eat it too. Here are a few secrets I kept to myself: I would binge on sugar and then head to the gym and do the StairMaster for an hour to compensate. I wouldn't eat all day, and then I'd eat right before going to bed. I would go all day long with barely one glass of water.

As my awareness expanded and my desire to live authentically grew, I knew I had to take a good look at all areas of life and make improvements. If I was teaching this stuff, it was becoming more important than ever to be congruent. If I was helping someone overcome their eating addictions, then I had to address my own.

Everything has to match up to vibrate out a magnet of truth and authenticity.

My first office was in a medical weight-loss center, and clients came to see me to work on the mindset piece. When I met Marie she was 100 pounds overweight and had tried a long laundry list of diets without success. My goal was to uncover her "why." Why would she want to live a healthy and vibrant life? Who did she love and what would she be willing to do for them (if not herself)? She immediately told the story about her amazing son, the one she loved with her entire heart.

That is the key. Focus on your *why* and not the *how*. Marie would do anything for her son. She would even learn to love, honor, and respect herself if it meant a better life for him. Seventy-five pounds down and six months later, Marie was at the gym for the first time in her life. Everything shifted, including the way she felt in her clothes. If you feel good in your skin, you know it. Start with the exercise that I gave to Marie when we first met. Look in the mirror and gaze deeply into your soul. Say out loud, "I love, honor, and respect me. I am worthy. I matter. My destiny is to have a strong and healthy body."

By the way, my big WHY is YOU. The world needs more brilliant, alive, and awakened people who are ready to shine just like you.

TIMELESS

My Destiny Is to Be Timeless
My Destiny Is to Be Ageless
My Destiny Is to Be Boundless
My Destiny Is to Be Limitless

Is it too late or can you live a life that is vibrant and full regardless of your age, bank account, or circumstance? If one person can do it, then it is possible.

When I first woke up to this possibility, I really didn't have any role models who were directly in my life, so I borrowed them. I thought, *What if I study those who have overcome similar obstacles and "pretend" them into my life?* And so it began. I was reciting my Destiny Power Statements daily, and I started to become aware of those who had blazed the trail before me. Marianne Williamson became my icon. I started studying *A Course in Miracles*. I began to feel a slowing down of time, an expansion of possibilities beyond limits, and a freedom from age and circumstance boundaries.

That exists for you too. It all starts as a thought. Everything is created twice, first as a thought and then as a reality. If you can conceive it and believe it with every cell in your body, then you can achieve it. You only use about 10% of your brainpower. The same is true for everyone. Now, think about the combined effect of sharing, masterminding, and combining all of those thoughts along with more brainpower. The results would be infinite.

Think about all of the successful people who are doing amazing things on both ends of the age spectrum—both the very young and those beyond midlife. Anything is possible at anytime. If a college student like Mark Zuckerberg can start Facebook or a major book publisher like Louise Hay can learn to ballroom dance in her eighties, then those opportunities exist for you too. You aren't too young or too old to make it happen.

Your timeline has no start date or finish line. Your potential has no ceiling. Your life has no boundaries.

If someone would have told me ten years ago I would be an author, speaker, coach, and spiritual teacher who leads people around the world on transformational retreats, I would have never believed that could be true. Inside of you is something as profound and wonderful for your life also.

I know it to be true because I experienced it, and I want you to know it too.

STRONG

My Destiny Is to Be Strong
My Destiny Is to Be Powerful
My Destiny Is to Be Courageous
My Destiny Is to Be Fearless

I met Pam at one of the local retreats I held in South Florida a few years back and then again recently in Bali for another. I knew of her story, but I didn't really know the heart and soul of this amazingly courageous woman who had lost her daughter to suicide until we spent time on the other side of the world together. Pam's daughter had been a junior in high school when their lives were forever changed.

One morning, Pam was in the kitchen preparing breakfast for the family when she sent her husband, Cesar, to open the locked door to Bailey's bedroom. When she heard Cesar screaming, she ran upstairs and found him holding their beautiful daughter's lifeless body in his arms. Pam could not look at her daughter's face, but written all over her body in green marker were the words "I'm sorry."

Pam untangled the power cord that Bailey had used to hang herself and called 911. Pam kept saying to herself, "Breathe, be present, breathe."

Pam felt the entire weight of the world on her shoulders. Everything moved in slow motion. One of many conversations Pam had following her daughter's death was with a doctor at UM. While she and the doctor spoke, a black and yellow butterfly kept flying by. In those moments, Pam could feel Bailey's presence and her love. The second day after Bailey's transition, the detectives released the letters Bailey had written to every one of her family members, teammates, and best friends. Her letters were sweet and funny, saying goodbye and expressing that she had been depressed for about a year. What Pam didn't know was how much Bailey had disliked herself and how much she blamed herself for all of the conflicts in her life.

There is a lot of pressure on juniors in high school who are trying to get an athletic scholarship. Bailey had been a great athlete. She had scored a 34 out of 36 on her ACT, high enough to get a soccer scholarship. The two weeks prior to her death, Bailey spent time touring Princeton, Clemson, and Dartmouth. All of these schools were interested in recruiting her. Bailey seemed awesome at living her life. She was good at everything—cooking, art, sports, school, fashion, etc. She continued to feel pressure to be better and felt that she fell short. Bailey had had no diagnosis, which could have potentially saved her life.

Mental health challenges in our youth requires awareness, and Pam has taken on that charge. She has started speaking in the community and has launched a program for suicide awareness in Bailey's high school. She courageously forges ahead to be a spokesperson on this often brushed-under-the-rug topic.

Over the last few years, I have openly talked about having had suicidal thoughts. My grandfather had committed suicide when I was young, and no one ever talked about it. There is a tendency to "pretend it away," but it exists and is way more common than is publically noted. On a regular basis, someone will approach me after I speak to share his or her own struggle with similar thoughts.

One of the powerful tools I used in my own life

to overcome my secret thoughts around suicide is called "Future Destiny Scripting." It wasn't until I could see myself healthy, happy, and free that I was able to start to feel some relief from the constant struggle of my thoughts. I had to rewrite my story by deleting stories that weren't really true but were ingrained deeply into my subconscious mind—the voice that told me that I didn't matter, I wasn't good enough, and my life had no value.

You can do this too by writing out your future story in detail the way you wish it was if you could design it. It is important to add power to the words by speaking them out loud. It is also important to record them so that you can listen over and over again to train your mind to have new, uplifting, positive thoughts. With repetition, you can replace the old dialogue and create new neural pathways in your brain and actually reshape it. This is an area of science I have been studying for the last three years, because it worked in my life. I went from feeling very unlucky to feeling very grateful and very fortunate. This area of science is called neuroplasticity. If you have experienced hopelessness, sadness, or pain in your life, you can rewire your brain with this technique, which will forever change your life and destiny.

GREEN

My Destiny Is to Go Green
My Destiny Is to Honor the Planet
My Destiny Is to See the Beauty
in Nature
My Destiny Is to Love Mother Earth

Most of life is lived indoors. Generations ago, our ancestors didn't live this way, but over time less and less of our time has been spent outdoors. What if your greatest freedom is so simple and obvious that it has become invisible to the eye? There is abundance and beauty everywhere, but most people are too busy to notice. When was the last time you got up to watch the sunrise or stopped to soak in all of the green lushness of nature while walking to your car? When was the last time you looked up at the sky and said, "I am unlimited just like the infinite blue up above"? If it has been a while, I suspect you would be a bit happier if you did.

I didn't start really watching the sunrise until my destiny shift occurred. Instead, I would go to the beach and chat on the phone. I would take a walk outside and think about my to-do list. I would walk through a garden and be focused on work. I wasn't really present, so most of what I saw was a fraction of what was in front of me. I wasn't letting all of Mother Earth's beauty inside of me. But boy, when I did, her trees came alive, every body of water sparkled, and the birds sang just for me. Nature wants you to notice her too. She wants to help you discover your divine destiny.

When I met my partner, Paul, he took me for a walk down along the sidewalk next to the beach in Delray Beach, Florida. He instructed me to stop and look at the green in the sea grapes . . . just to stop and soak it in. I was blissing out with this request, but it was early in our relationship, so I remained cool, while thinking quietly to myself, *Hmm . . . he's caught my attention.*

Then on our next date, he asked me to look up at the infinite, limitless blue sky. *Really, are you kidding me?* I said to myself. I must have manifested someone superspecial for him to be connected to Mother Earth as deeply as he was.

Moving forward, Paul's story wasn't a big surprise to me when I learned more. At twenty-two, he was working in construction when he felt enormous pain in his head. He was rushed to the hospital. The testing quickly revealed that he had a cerebral hemorrhage. They drilled a hole in his skull to relieve the pressure while he waited to be stabilized enough for surgery. Paul could not have any brain stimulation, so he was placed in a dark room by himself for the following three months leading up to surgery. Paul never knew if he would ever return home again. He was blessed with a successful procedure and was able to finally go home with full vision and his life back.

Life throws curve balls. Experiencing a brush with death at an early age redefines one's priorities. But it doesn't have to happen after you get a diagnosis. You can live that abundance and richness right now.

One of the many games Paul and I like to play is "How many leaves are on that tree? How many blades of grass are in that field? How many colors are alive in nature?" We ask such questions and then just start observing, noticing the abundance everywhere.

Mother Nature is sending you messages through her beauty all day long. She is alive and wants to be acknowledged and loved. For every thought vibration of appreciation that you send to her, she blesses our entire planet with appreciation right back. Cool, right?

GIVING

My Destiny Is to Be Generous and Giving
My Destiny Is to Share and Help People
My Destiny Is to Be of Service to Others
My Destiny Is to Make a Difference
in the World

I used to believe that participation in charities was meant for those who were lucky enough to have lots of time, money, and resources to give away. If someone asked for a charitable donation, I would write a small check, feel good about doing something, and carry on. That was until I hit one of the lowest points in my life.

I had lived most of my life thinking about ending my life. I never really felt like I fit in and certainly didn't feel like I offered much value in the world. I had low self-esteem and struggled with depression.

At that point in my life, I was barely speaking to my mom; my two boys, Daniel and Cory, who were fifteen and sixteen, wanted little to do with me; and everywhere I turned was drama and chaos. However, once I'd looked into the eyes of my children, I knew suicide was not an option. So there I was: doing so much for everyone in my life to make up for something. But that clearly wasn't working. I even suspected that it could be making it worse.

That is when I decided to go in reverse. Instead of doing more for the direct people in my life, I decided to find someone who didn't really have support and give that person my time, energy, and money. That week, I spotted a flyer at Starbucks that outlined a program called "Take Stock in Children," and that is exactly what I did.

When I met Jonathan I fell instantly in love with the new addition to my family. He was in tenth grade and was part of a state-sponsored program that would provide college scholarships for kids who were considered low income and at risk and had scored well on an entrance exam in the sixth grade. I believe that I got even more out of the program than Jonathan did. I kept my involvement private and didn't even mention it to my family for at least the first year. I met Jonathan every Friday for two years, and although there were times that he almost didn't make it through, in the end, he graduated and got his scholarship.

He took a city bus to school each day across town and got in early to prepare the school breakfast, which meant he was able to eat for free. He worked at night and pitched in financially at home to help out his mom. His girlfriend gave birth prematurely to their daughter his senior year. And through it all, Jonathan taught me the power of giving back in such a profound way that I will never ever be the same. The blessings he gave me reshaped me, and I am so grateful.

Most recently, his mom came to one of my retreats, and she has also changed her life. Evelyn watched what I did to help her son, so she decided to go back to school and inspire others in the same way. The effect of kindness, caring, and making a difference is contagious.

Nothing can shift a perspective faster than helping someone else through a difficult time. Now whenever I feel blue or out of sorts, I go do something for someone else. I do it for them, and in the long run, I benefit even more. I feel blessed to know this. I plan to continue to spread the word.

RICH LIFE

My Destiny Is to Live a Rich Life
My Destiny Is to See Abundance
Everywhere
My Destiny Is to Be Prosperous
My Destiny Is to Live and Be Free

If you ask ten different people to describe wealth, you would probably get ten different answers in response. Some would say health is wealth, or it is having their children close by. Some would say it's millions in the bank, and others would equate it with assets, including owning homes, a luxury boat, and lots of travel. It all depends on one's personal perspective.

The last few years as a coach has reinforced a life lesson that everyone already knows intellectually.

It further infused my desire to do this work at an even bigger level. Here it is:

Money is energy. Money itself does not equate to happiness. It never has and never will. The root of happiness exists inside your heart, not in your bank account. I was making a good income in the pharmaceutical industry when I was compelled to leave to start my coaching, speaking, and writing profession. I have never looked back. I had to leave that occupation to be congruent with my new beliefs. That part of me knows that inside of you is a healthy and whole person, even if the doctor told you otherwise, even if your test results say something different. It is just up to you to do the work to shift your perspective so that you can make important changes that will dramatically add more health wealth into your bank account.

I am humbly grateful that I live in abundance every day when I see the sunrise and the sunset, when I walk through nature, and each day that I am still alive. You have that wealth. It is inside of you. It is your gold. And it is abundantly flowing, even if your bank account doesn't reflect it just yet. Start with your inhale and notice the abundance of air all around you. Bless your money. Thank your bills for providing you electric, phone service, and housing. Acknowledge the overflow in all areas of your life.

Craig came into my life as a client through the yoga world and is a shining example of how money and happiness sometimes take a zigzag road before they intersect. He was a fast-paced executive in the world of finances and sixty pounds overweight with a bank account full of stress and heaviness.

Then one day his doctor gave him the big news, and it wasn't that he was going to open a new investment account. He gave him the "you better change your life or else you are risking your future" talk. Calculating risk was Craig's forte, and this time he got it. He jumped into yoga reluctantly at first but was lucky enough to find two yogi diamonds who helped him find his way: Mary Ann and Leslie.

The fascinating thing about change is that it trickles over to all areas of your life. Craig shifted his business model too and now works with women who are going through a transition, helping them the same way Mary Ann and Leslie had helped him. He now feels compelled to share his strategic knowledge of growing both more happiness and wealth.

RELEASE

My Destiny Is to Release
My Destiny Is to Let Go
My Destiny Is to Surrender
My Destiny Is to Set Myself Free

I never really considered myself a hoarder. I thought I was just unlucky and stuck with stuff that happened to me through unfortunate circumstance. I certainly had no idea I could actually clear energy and release it. I didn't remember ever taking a course on "forgiving and letting go" in school.

Now, once I became aware that it was possible, it certainly didn't mean it was going to be easy. Whew, okay, at least there was hope, which was all I needed to fuel my desire.

I had three-plus people in my life who, when I thought about them, would create a cascade of really negative feelings that would flood my body with emotions like fear, anger, despair, sadness, hopelessness, and anxiety, just to name a few.

Okay, I knew who they were and how I felt about them, but how was I going to do this "release thing"? One thing I knew for sure was that if I could forgive them and then ask for forgiveness for anyone whose list I might be on, then I would be clearing space for miracles and blessings. I'd heard Marianne Williamson say this, and something inside of me knew her words to be true. That was the first big step. So I ranked each person on the list, making a decision to do the easiest of the three first. Almost every day, I would send that person love, light, and blessings for one to two minutes. I really didn't want to and came up with almost every excuse in the book why I didn't have to do it, but I did it anyway because that little whispering voice told me that if I could, then all of the pain I was feeling would go away. I was desperate for relief.

You know this process works when you think of that person and suddenly feel totally neutral about them. Not good or bad, just neutral. This happened for me with the first person on my list. Keep in mind that it isn't necessary to love that person, bring them back into your life, or continue the process once you know the work is complete.

The second one was trickier. I had to tap into a new level of desire. I pretended this person was my son as an adult, and I was his mother. I felt the unconditional love a mother feels for her child even if they have done something to hurt another and was able to open my heart to forgiveness. It took close to a year, but I was able to free my soul of those chains too.

Then came the last person, and it was a doozy for me. It was tough, and I didn't want to do it. That is where I used a strategy that I still share today. I set my alarm on my phone for 3 pm, and every day at the same time, I would pause and send love, light, and blessings. Boy, was it challenging.

The interesting part was no one knew I was doing this, including the people I was forgiving. They had no idea all of this was going on in my head. The only prisoner was me, and I was setting myself free. A year later, I knew the curse was broken. I released it. And if I can do it, so can you.

Lori carried the burden of a past relationship when we first met a friend's dinner party. I mentioned that I lead a "live" intention setting on the beach once a week, and the following week she was there. Lori did the release work. She showed up every week, started private coaching with me, and even traveled to Bali with my retreat partner, Leslie, and me. She even created a Release candle, since her health and wellness business carries a paraffin candle line to help others through the same process.

Creating a ritual, such as lighting a Release candle and/or setting a daily timer, helps you stay true to the process. This is how habits are created. Releasing isn't something you do once, and it is done. It is a continuous process of forgiving and letting go.

What if your entire life is a practice zone to help you learn to let go so at the very end of life you can transition with love and grace? Why not set your alarm for 3:00 pm right now and join the thousands of people who are using this same process. You can sign up at www.4giveat3.com and start today. You can choose to be finally free.

CONFIDENT

My Destiny Is to Be Confident
My Destiny Is to Take Risks
My Destiny Is to Do Something New
My Destiny Is to Set a Big,
Hairy Audacious Goal

Most people live in the middle. They don't want to stand out or take on too much, fearing the unknown. I was one of them. I created my story from the time I was a young girl: I would go to school, get a job, have a family, and live happily ever after.

Really? Who came up with that storyline? It didn't even enter my mind that there were other options. I followed the pack. I looked around to see where the crowd was heading, and I got right in line without asking any questions. I automatically just tagged along.

And then one day, I had a new awareness. It started first when I applied to the pharmaceutical industry and actually got the job and had to bust through my story that I wasn't smart enough to get a doctor to listen to what I had to say. I only mastered that because I had to as a single mom, supporting my family. I thought I had no choice.

Then I had to leave an abusive relationship after 9-11 expanded my awareness. Life can be taken away in an instant; knowing that gave me more confidence. That day empowered me. I couldn't let go of the thought that the people who died had no choice. But I did. I decided to live more confidently in honor of the lives that were lost.

I wasn't much on taking risk. That is why I followed the herd. I thought it was safer there. Boy, is that upside down. When you stay on the sidelines, you risk really living a rich life. But then I hit the lottery. I discovered a Universal Truth. You can change your destiny, but you have to build your confidence, take risks, do something different, and start setting goals. It all starts as a thought. Then with some effort, it can become a reality.

Hilary came my way by happenstance. She saw a flyer for one of my events and felt drawn to it like a magnet. It was out of the box for Hilary, but somehow she mustered up the courage and stepped into this new life-changing experience. The weekend spoke to her, but she still knew that to get the big breakthroughs, she needed more. Hilary came to stay at my private home for one-on-one intensives several times over the course of two years, plus a number of other interactions. I even picked her up since she was fearful of driving on the highway. This was a big stretch for Hilary, so I was willing. Then it happened: she set a big, hairy audacious goal. She quietly whispered, "I want to go to Bali with you." Now this was a girl who didn't want to drive one hour north by herself on the highway, speaking out a big dream.

I decided to give her a gentle nudge. "How much money do you have in your wallet?" I asked her. She replied, "Fifty bucks."

I said, "Saying yes means giving me what you have to show the Universe you mean business." And you know the rest of the story . . . Hilary is a traveling rock star and so much more.

Today, decide to do something totally out of character. Find something that makes your heart sing and set a big, hairy audacious goal around it.

BELIEVE

My Destiny Is to Believe
My Destiny Is to Have Faith
My Destiny Is to Trust
My Destiny Is to Have
Unwavering Certainty

Up until a few years ago, I believed that my whole life was one big mistake and that I should have never been born. I believed that somehow I got picked to be unlucky in this lifetime, and that was just the way it was. I felt victimized. I had little faith and believed my future was doomed. I saw no way out. Then a miracle happened. I opened up to a new possibility just when I was about to give up entirely on life.

Then one day, I had a new thought. It burst through my old belief system. I had nothing to lose, so I tested it out. The part of me that felt comfortable with clinical data decided to look at these new ideas like an experiment. What if my beliefs were wrong? What if everything I have known to be true wasn't? And then it happened. New beliefs started to form. I received validation from the Universe immediately in the way of coincidences and synchronicity. I took notice. I started to connect the patterns as if life were a big jigsaw puzzle, and I started to see how it all meshed together. I saw how all the dots connected. I continued to explore, and with a flashlight in hand, I had a new awareness.

What if instead of seeing it *after* you believe it, you see it *when* you believe it. I researched, tested, and confirmed that to be true. It is in all religious and spiritual teachings, and this Universal Law was proving itself to be true in my own life.

Now this has become my personal motto. I wear a bracelet that says faith, and I touch it often. I have had to grow into this level of belief, but now I have so much conviction around the power of believing that it has overflowed enough for both of us. Everything doesn't always happen the exact way you want it to happen, but if you believe long and deep enough, it will happen even bigger and better.

Start small building this muscle so that you can

see it in action, fueling your belief even more. Set goals, meditate on them, forgive the people in your life who have hurt you, breathe in the abundance of Mother Nature, send blessings out randomly as a way to give back, connect with your center, love with a gigantic heart, be authentic, and do random acts of kindness. Vibrate your higher thoughts, and always no matter what, believe.

If you haven't ever explored your personal beliefs, start making a list. What do you believe to be true? Now begin asking yourself, "What if that belief isn't true?" Just for fun, test out a new belief, and just observe what happens. It is my experience that this is one of the main ingredients to creating a new destiny.

LEARN

My Destiny Is to Learn
My Destiny Is to Grow
My Destiny Is to Become More
My Destiny Is to Be a Lifelong Student

I went to college to get out of the house. When I was a teenager, I'd watched my mom struggle as a waitress just to pay the bills. I believed that going to school was the golden ticket to a better job and eventually a good life. I was willing to work and pay my way to get my degree and do whatever it took to be independent, self-sufficient, and free.

Well, it didn't exactly happen that way. My follow-the-herd mentally took me right to business school, which is where I randomly picked my finance degree based on how much money I believed I could earn. Don't get me wrong. I see life as a big jigsaw puzzle and every piece an integrate part of the whole, and this was the right decision for me at the time. Every part of life layers an important aspect of "self" on top of the other. Looking back, the interesting part was that my heart yearned to be a school teacher who would open a dance/yoga studio after she retired. Instead, I followed the herd to where I believed the money was: in business school. It all intersects.

Flash-forward thirty years later. The last decade is where my real learning occurred. It all started with an opening, a burning desire to dissect every aspect of life—to obsessively study success, science, and spirituality and how they merged together. After twenty-five years of launching medications for various diseases in the pharmaceutical industry, I had learned how to intently study, analyze, and observe clinical studies. This was a skill set I took with me when I began studying the meaning of life. I had become analytical, and I somehow finally believed that I was teachable enough to absorb it all.

When the student is ready, the teacher will appear. And so many of them did. I started my new course of study with three books: *The Artist Way* by Julia Cameron, *A Course in Miracles* by the Foundation for Inner Peace, and *The Power of Your Subconscious Mind* by Joseph Murphy.

In the world of Big Pharma, every year we had to take a big test. We had to score a 90% or better, or we would be put on probation. If we didn't pass on the next go-around, we would lose our job. As a single mom, I was petrified that might happen, so I studied like crazy. This strong study ethic pai off. I studied these new books like my life depended on it.

I also started following spiritual and success thought leaders such as Marianne Williamson, Michael Beckwith, and Gabrielle Bernstein. I studied their journey and style. I was hungry for knowledge, and the more I learned, the more I inspired I was to learn more.

Now, in the version of myself that I know is my *why I am,* I have arrived home. I have immense gratitude for those brilliant minds and loving hearts who have spent their valuable time, love, and money sharing their wisdom through their books. Five years ago, I didn't personally know any authors, but now I know hundreds of dedicated and phenomenal authors.

You don't know what you don't know until you know it. I had to learn this truth, which is why it speaks to me so deeply.

VISUALIZE

My Destiny Is to Visualize
My Destiny Is to Believe
My Destiny Is to Vibrate
My Destiny Is to Manifest

When I first heard someone referred to as a visionary, I wasn't sure what it meant. I had to pause and reflect on the word. I guess I had heard the term used before to describe Martin Luther King, Jr., and a few other great leaders, but I had no idea that inside each one of us exists a visionary. The only difference is whether the "visionary" switch is on or off—like a light switch on the wall.

As a child, the switch is in the "on" position and takes the form of imagination, pretending, and playing dress-up. Then someone tells you to get serious and stop pretending to be someone you are not, so you turn your switch off. You become influenced by someone else's viewpoint of who you should or shouldn't be. Your light of potential diminishes.

So here is the deal. Your switch is still inside of you. It's there. You can turn it back on. It will take practice and perhaps a guide to help you, but you *can* do it. Everything is created twice, first as a thought. The substance of a thought becomes a feeling, which vibrates a frequency out into the world that attracts a similar vibration in the form of manifestation back into your experience.

When I first learned about this stuff, it blew my mind. *Just start thinking a thought, and it will manifest?* I became a student of this process and got my certification in neuro-linguistic programming (NLP) and hypnosis. Again, the years I spent studying for my profession paid off, and I dove deeply into the study of neuroplasticity—a miraculous process by which the brain reorganizes its neural connections in response to new circumstances and environments and then remodels itself. I knew somewhere I would find the link between science and spirituality, and there it was.

Each time you think a thought, you are creating a new neuron. We think the same thought pattern throughout the day over and over again, which creates grooves in our brain, releasing chemicals into our bloodstream like dopamine and serotonin. Wow, so you think a new thought and condition the mind to repeat the new thought over and over again, and you create a new groove and rewire your brain? This is real documented stuff. I could really sink my mind into this.

I felt like I hit the lotto, once again.

Now, layer that with the knowledge that you are made of energy, a vibrating machine that emits an electromagnetic frequency out from within. Everything around you is made up of energy and emits a frequency also. So you are a human magnet, pulsating a vibe at all times. They can be good vibes or not-so-good vibes. And it all takes place within the communication between your feeling heart and your thinking mind. Those two organs are exchanging information, which creates your vibrational field.

Now let's bring it back home. Most people think in pictures, so when you visualize something that you want and can focus your attention on it, then you are thinking thoughts about it too, right? Those thoughts are mixed with emotions, hopefully gratitude and happiness, that become your feelings. Those feelings send an energetic wave out into the Universe infused with a set level of power (wattage) based on your personal level of belief, faith, and trust. The stronger your belief that it will happen, the stronger the current. That is why some people seem to manifest at a greater frequency than others. Everyone has this ability.

Can I keep quiet about this discovery? No way. I taught myself to become a public speaker, how to write books, how to create products, how to become an entrepreneur, how to market, send newsletters, etc., so that I can share this powerful message with millions of people around the globe. I am on a BIG mission. And I want you to spread the word too.

My Personal Vision involves you. I ask you to boldly share this book and message with as many people as you can. The Power of One can change one. That is all it takes. You are a divine being with infinite potential, and you are the one. If you are reading this, it is your time to shine. Your light is illuminating.

I see your bright light. I hold the space with you. I believe you are magnificent beyond your imagination. I can feel your energy vibrating your specialness, talents, and gifts.

I know you are manifesting greatness in this very instant. Join me in that vision. Believe it is your birthright. Vibrate out your true essence. Manifest your new story, future, life.

THE SEED

My Destiny Is to Plant the Seeds
My Destiny Is to Water the Soil
My Destiny Is to Be Patient
My Destiny Is to Have Faith
and Just Know

Everything starts as a seed. Life starts as a seed. A forest starts as a single seed that becomes many. Even physical objects start as seeds. Yes, even the chair you are sitting on! Everything is created first as the seed of a thought, and then, if that thought is put into motion and cultivated, that idea manifests in the world. Every person you meet comes into your life for a reason that can potentially grow into a beautiful garden—one seed at a time.

One such seed in my life is Mary Ann. She had requested to meet several years ago through a client I was coaching, who was one of the fitness experts in the gym where she worked. Both the gym and another clothing store in the plaza carried my inspirational clothing line called "What Is Your Destiny," and Mary Ann had loved the shirts. She had just completed a 200-hour yoga certification training, and Mary Ann wore one of them for her graduation.

At our first meeting, I was struck by her kind words and how enthusiastic she was to get together. Mary Ann left a lasting impression on me as one of the most sincere, open, kind, and heart-centered people I had ever met. I knew that my meeting with Mary Ann was divinely orchestrated. She has been one of the most important seeds in my life since day one.

If we go backward and trace the generations on our family tree, we see how many sprout from the seeds of just two. When we go back far enough, we realize that we all come from the same source. Just soak that in for a moment. Many people "unremember" because so many layers of people, circumstances, and life happen on top of it, and then it becomes easy to forget—not intentionally, of course. It is just human nature to want to remember the thing that happened right before the end result.

But there would be no harvest if the farmer hadn't prepared the soil and planted the seeds in the fertile ground. It is powerful to, just for a moment, go back and recall the origins.

Mary Ann started to coach with me while building her brand and her business several years ago. I loved working with her because she was so compassionate, loving, and open. She worked diligently to help her yoga clients get real results—emotionally, physically, and spiritually.

During this time, I experienced a setback in my own life, and I was on the verge of another metamorphosis. From expanding my business to moving on from my marriage, this was a very difficult time in my life. What I did have, but didn't realize at the time, was a wonderful bounty in my garden growing from the original introduction to Mary Ann.

I had been organizing weekend retreats twice a year that focused on self-development and reprogramming the subconscious mind. I asked Mary Ann to be one of the yoga teachers at the retreats. Although she was new as a teacher, my intuition said, "She is the one." You just know sometimes, and it is in that knowing that your greatest validations take place. When you trust your heart and your gut, it always turns out "right." Not only did

Mary Ann say yes, but everyone who attended the retreats totally loved her. In addition to yoga, she shared her loving, caring, and beautiful heart. Mary Ann was *just right*.

I was and continue to be blessed to have Mary Ann in my life. From that first seed, so many more have been planted. Mary Ann, along with the other phenomenal teachers and workshop leaders, has contributed to all of the success of the retreats. And there is so much more.

When someone is generous and thoughtful (for example, Mary Ann), they often think about how they can share, help, and support others. I have met the most incredible people through Mary Ann. When she shared with me that she was pursuing her 500-hour yoga teacher certification, I decided to do it too. I even made a decision to move to Delray to be close to the Yoga community in this area. I finally feel like this is it, and I am home where I belong, a feeling I have been searching for in my heart for a very long time.

To know Mary Ann is to love her. She is one of those special people who inspire me. I am so blessed and grateful to have her in my life.

Each one of us is planting seeds in our own garden and in the gardens of others. You never know whose life you have touched or how many layers of gardens have grown because of a kind word you have said, a smile you have shared, or a helping hand you have given someone. You don't do it for the recognition because, most of the time, someone isn't going to write about it in a book. You do it because that is who you are.

You were born with a seed, and you are continuously planting them whether you realize it or not. Every thought you think has the power to change the world. Your imagination (aka thoughts) are *that* powerful. You may not be the one who does it directly, but you might inspire someone who inspires someone else, and they might be the one who does the work. But you did yours by planting the seed. You are the farmer. Your work is the original seed.

Close your eyes and envision planting a seed. Place it deep into the ground. Now imagine the rain sprinkling over it. See the sun shining down to give it life. See the bud breaking through the soil. Allow your inner eye to see an oak tree form—first one and then two and three, even four trees, all standing beside that original tree. Now see an entire forest , rich with green vibrancy , health, and beauty. See yourself sitting under the first tree and feel the immense love and gratitude that is in your heart right now. You are the seed. You planted the seed. The seed continues to expand into more and more goodness. And so it is.

It is my wish and desire for this book to be one of your seeds.

APPENDICES

BREATHING EXERCISE

Breathing is the first thing you do when you are born and the last thing you will do before you transition. The breath is life in its purist form. Focusing on the breath provides an instant way to release stress and replace it with a state of calm and tranquility. It is simple, and with these basic steps, you can get started immediately. By the way, you can do this anywhere anytime. My favorite place to do this breath work is in my car, and many times, I do it while I am driving.

- Take a deep inhale through your nose to a count of 4, hold for a count of 4, and then exhale to a count of 4. Repeat 4 times.

- Next, inhale to a count of 6, hold for a count of 6, and then exhale to a count of 6. Repeat 6 times.

- Allow all the tension to release with each exhale, and inhale complete peace and serenity.

You can also incorporate a power phrase or word while doing your breath work. Here are a few examples:

- Inhale to a count of 4 while focusing on inner peace. Hold peace and tranquility for a count of 4. Then, release to a count of 4 as you focus on removing any chaos or drama in your life.

- Inhale to a count of 4 while focusing on the essence of love. At the top of that breath, hold unconditional love. Then, release to a count of 4 as you focus on removing any and all fear, knowing you are always divinely loved.

- Inhale to a count of 4 while focusing on joy and happiness. Hold a smile deep within your heart for a count of 4. Then, release to a count of 4 as you focus on removing any and all sadness, worry, or stress.

One of the reasons I believe that the power of breath work is not commonly referenced or recommended by the medical community or other big corporate powers of change is because it is free. You really can't charge people for air. I came from the pharmaceutical industry and was blown away by how effective breath work was to lower blood pressure, so effective that many people can be taken off of their medications. The crazy part of this equation is that after I gave my resignation, I was asked to teach these techniques to nurses and doctors at the same hospitals by the hospitals themselves that I had been calling on professionally to sell the medications. Interesting, right?

MEDITATION

Meditation can be intimidating. The minute you decide to try it out and close your eyes to go within, your mind will start to race. Be gentle with yourself and go slow. Start in any comfortable position. I began my journey into meditation in my car by parking in a lot under a tree and closing my eyes for 5–10 minutes. I just focused on my breath. My mind fought me every step of the way. I came up with a zillion excuses, such as "I don't have time for this." What I eventually realized is the busier you are, the more you need meditation. It's a paradox, as much of life is.

Find a quiet place where you won't be interrupted. I even meditated in my walk-in closet so that my family wouldn't roll their eyes at me or see what I was doing. I kept my meditation a secret for a couple of years before I was comfortable enough to share it. You can begin with 5–10 minutes of silent time in a private space. Simply follow the steps below:

- Get comfortable in a cross-legged position, in a chair, or lying down. Start to breathe in through your nose, deeply inhaling and exhaling.

- Slowly begin to visualize the color red. See it swirling around and getting brighter and brighter. Imagine this brilliant ruby-red light filling your entire body. Now focus on a red rose. See an entire room filled with red roses and smell the beautiful scent of the rose petals. With your mind's eye, see the richness of the texture and imagine feeling the softness of each petal. Feel the sensation of softness in your body.

- Now see the color change to orange—a brilliant, beautiful bright orange getting brighter and brighter. Inhale the aroma of oranges while gazing inward, pulsating and vibrating the color of orange sherbet.

- Now see the color change to yellow, a yellow as bright as the sun rising in the morning over the horizon. Feel the warmth of this bright golden light pouring over your entire body. Allow this sparkle of sunshine to fill every one of your cells until they are all pulsating this yellow light.

- Now see the color change to green. Imagine being in a lush, green tropical oasis surrounded by nature. Inhale the rich scent of evergreens. See the abundance of leaves on the trees and feel the aliveness of Mother Earth sprinkling her green essence everywhere.

- Now see the color change to blue as you look up at the boundless, limitless sky. There is blue everywhere—a beautiful, soft blue skyward and the blue of the expansive ocean before you. Feel the coolness of water as you walk along the beach at the water's edge. Feel the breeze on your skin, and see your entire body merging with this blue light and filling your body with a sense of peace, calmness, and tranquility.

- Now see the color change to purple as you inhale the scent of lavender all around you. Imagine running through a field of lavender with your arms wide open. You feel expansive and light. You feel a powerful connection to everything and everyone. This purple light is sparkling and shining all around you.

- Now see the color change to the brightest light of all—an iridescent white sparkling light that shines all over you. This light shimmers its brilliance to awaken you to your true essence of divine light. This pure twinkling energy of light moves into your physical body and coats every one of your cells with diamonds of light. They sparkle goodness and shine blessings into your life. You are always surrounded by this light. You are this light. Now and always.

- Allow the vortex of peace, love, and freedom to vibrate inward by sitting quietly for an additional 5 minutes. You can add to this reflection time in 5-minute increments to eventually reach a total of 20 minutes or beyond. Do this once or twice a day.

TIP: After reading the above, gently close your eyes for reflection time. Don't get discouraged if other thoughts pop into your head. Just gently watch them float by without judgment and then return to where you left off when you can. When I started my own practice, it took six months to a year before I could get close to actually emptying my mind. It still continues to be a practice that I must, well, practice.

PRAYERS

Once I gave myself permission to let go of the label "prayer" so that I could redefine for myself what "prayer" means, I discovered its incredible power. I share below a few of my favorites that are simple and straight to the point. I really got excited when I realized that I didn't have to go to a religious center to pray and that I could make my sacred place under a tree. That really resonated with me! This one prayer became my daily mantra:

> *It is with much love and gratitude that I come before the Divine Universe to ask for divine guidance and protection—physically, emotionally, spiritually, and financially. I stand in complete faith and believe in the power of prayer. Peace and joy to all.*

You can use this prayer to connect to
your angels:

Angels around us
Angels beside us
Angels above us
Angels within us
Angels are watching over us.
Thank you, my dear angels.

You can use this prayer for divine protection:

Light is around us
Light is beside us
Light is above us
Light is below us
Light is within us
Light shines on us.
Thank you for sharing the light.

You can use this prayer for divine love:

Love is around us
Love is beside us
Love is above us
Love is below us
Love is within us
Love is all there is
Thank you for expanding my heart.

You can use this prayer for divine peace:

Peace is around us
Peace is beside us
Peace is above us
Peace is below us
Peace is within us
Peace is everywhere
Thank you for the gift of peace.

DESTINY POWER WORDS

A   Amazing, Awesome, Abundance, Authentic, Angels, Appreciative, Achievement, Allow, Acceptance, Alive, Art, Awaken, Awe

B   Beautiful, Blissful, Believe, Blessed, Balance, Blossom, Bountiful, Breathe, Bright, Brilliance

C   Calm, Clarity, Compassion, Courage, Creativity, Confidence, Consciousness, Cheerful, Curious

D   Delightful, Divine, Dream, Determination, Dazzle, Delicious, Dynamic

E   Energetic, Enhance, Expansion, Ease, Empower, Effortless, Embrace, Energy, Enjoy, Excitement

F   Fun, Friendly, Focus, Fearless, Freedom, Faith, Frequency, Fantastic, Forgiveness, Full

G   Great, Good, Gratitude, Generous, Giving, Growth, Giggle, Grace, Gentle, Groovy

H   Happiness, Harmony, Hugs, Honor, Humility, Health, Hope, Heal, Humanity

I   Innovation, Inspiration, Integrity Intuition, Improve, Inhale, Invigorate

J   Joy, Jolly, Jubilant, Jump, Jasmine

K   Kindness, Kiss, Kinetic

L   Love, Leadership, Light, Lucky, Limitless, Laugh, Lavender, Learn, Liberate, Listen

M   Mindfulness, Mindset, Magnetic, Manifest, Meaningful, Miracle, Music, Majestic

N   Non attachment, Nurture, Nature, Nourish, N

O   Oneness, Opportunity, Open, Overflowing, Optimistic

P   Pleasant, Passionate, Prosperity, Powerful, Purpose, Protection, Positivity, Playful, Patient, Peace

Q   Quiet, Quality

R   Relaxation, Resilient, Release, Receive, Radiant, Realize, Reflection, Refresh

S   Strong, Simply, Surrender, Success, Shine, Sincere, Sing, Soft, Sparkle, Special, Savor, Stretch

T   Thankful, Truth, Treasure, Thrill, Tickle, Tolerant, Thrive, Thoughtful, Transcend

U   Understanding, Unique, Us, Unfold, Unshakable, Uplifting, Useful

V   Victorious, Vibration, Visualization, Vitality, Validate, Valued, Vibrant

W   Wonderful, Wealth, Wellness, Warmth, Wonder, Worthy, Whole

Y   Yes, Yoga, Yummy, Youthful

Z   Zest, Zeal

DESTINY POWER STATEMENTS

MIRACLES

My Destiny Is to Believe in Miracles
My Destiny Is to Create Miracles
My Destiny Is to Receive Miracles
My Destiny Is to Be a Miracle

DESTINY

My Destiny Is to Be Peace
My Destiny Is to Be Calm
My Destiny Is to Be Centered
My Destiny Is to Be Balanced

GRATEFUL

My Destiny Is to Be Grateful
My Destiny Is to Be Thankful
My Destiny Is to Be Appreciative
My Destiny Is to Count My Blessings

BODY

My Destiny Is to Love My Body
My Destiny Is to Be Fit
My Destiny Is to Be Toned
My Destiny Is to Have a Strong and
    Healthy Body

TIMELESS

My Destiny Is to Be Timeless
My Destiny Is to Be Ageless
My Destiny Is to Be Boundless
My Destiny Is to Be Limitless

STRONG

My Destiny Is to Be Strong
My Destiny Is to Be Powerful
My Destiny Is to Be Courageous
My Destiny Is to Be Fearless

GREEN

My Destiny Is to Go Green
My Destiny Is to Honor the Planet
My Destiny Is to See the Beauty in Nature
My Destiny Is to Love Mother Earth

GIVING

My Destiny Is to Be Generous and Giving
My Destiny Is to Share and Help People
My Destiny Is to Be of Service to Others
My Destiny Is to Make a Difference in
    the World

RICH LIFE

My Destiny Is to Live a Rich Life
My Destiny Is to See Abundance
   Everywhere
My Destiny Is to Be Prosperous
My Destiny Is to Live and Be Free

RELEASE

My Destiny Is to Release
My Destiny Is to Let Go
My Destiny Is to Surrender
My Destiny Is to Set Myself Free

CONFIDENT

My Destiny Is to Be Confident
My Destiny Is to Take Risks
My Destiny Is to Do Something New
My Destiny Is to Set a Big, Hairy
   Audacious Goal

BELIEVE

My Destiny Is to Believe
My Destiny Is to Have Faith
My Destiny Is to Trust
My Destiny Is to Have Unwavering
  Certainty

LEARN

My Destiny Is to Learn
My Destiny Is to Grow
My Destiny Is to Become More
My Destiny Is to Be a Lifelong
  Student

VISUALIZE

My Destiny Is to Visualize
My Destiny Is to Believe
My Destiny Is to Vibrate
My Destiny Is to Manifest

I BELIEVE...

I believe that everything happens for a reason.

I believe there is good in everyone.

I believe anything is possible if you are willing to believe.

I believe you are never too old to start living a life you love.

I believe everyone has a story worth listening to.

I believe through our imagination anything is possible.

I believe when we forgive, we become light, happy, and free.

I believe everyone was born to shine.

I believe abundance is our birthright.

I believe laughter is the best medicine.

I believe that each new day is an opportunity to begin again.

I believe we are both a teacher and a student.

I believe our pain, difficulties, and challenges
   show up to awaken us.

I believe every thought is a powerful seed.

I believe emotional strength is a muscle that
   can be developed.

I believe meditation is a game changer.

I believe every man, woman, and child has gifts,
   talents, and uniqueness to share in the world.

I believe it is better to be kind than to be right

I believe if it is supposed to happen, it will, and
   if it doesn't, something even better is suppose
   to happen.

I believe in gratitude.

I believe anyone can change their mind, which
   in turn will change their circumstance.

I believe there is a powerful source of energy
   that wants to support and help us.

I believe in dreaming big.

I believe you often can heal your physical body
   by healing your emotional self.

I believe that a breakdown often precedes a
   breakthrough.

I believe that the real goal is happiness.

I believe if you love what you do, then others
   will feel your energy and love it too.

I believe in living out loud.

I believe that passion, persistence, and patience is the formula for success.

I believe that success starts in the mind.

I believe that it isn't *I'll believe it when I see it,* but *I will see it when I believe it.*

I believe in a higher power.

I believe we are the vessel and source is the supply.

I believe in the power of intention.

I believe that what you focus on truly does expand—both negative and positive.

I believe that you influence through the power of your words.

I believe that great leaders lead by example.

I believe that prayers do get answered.

I believe that gratitude brings more to be grateful for into your life.

I believe that one question can change your life.

I believe that the answer to less stress exists in the power of our breath.

I believe that peace in the world starts with peace in our own world.

I believe that we feel most alive when we are creating.

I believe we are all intuitive and that some of have just built that muscle stronger than others.

I believe that if it doesn't feel right in your gut you shouldn't do it.

I believe that what we eat should be made from mother earth and god.

I believe we are all brothers and sisters from the same family—humanity.

I believe your level of happiness can be increased just by spending more time in nature.

I believe that to sustain a high level of energy throughout one's lifetime, your battery needs to be recharged on a regular basis.

I believe that everything is energy, vibration, and frequency.

I believe in reverse engineering the creative process by seeing the end result first.

I believe that fear is a learned emotion that can be replaced with courage.

I believe that we don't know what we don't know.

I believe our imagination is one of our greatest gifts.

I believe that you can learn anything you set your mind to.

I believe in leaning into something new gradually.

I believe that we need time to process new information for it to stick.

I believe in all religion and no religion.

I believe in moving the body in some way every day.

I believe in stretching into uncomfortable.

I believe in declarations, autosuggestion, and affirmations.

I believe in the power of community and teamwork.

I believe in never giving up.

I believe the right people show up at the right time if you are open to receive them.

I believe in living in the moment.

I believe in training the brain and connecting to the heart.

I believe we are destined for greatness, and it is up to us to recognize it.

I believe the best is yet to come.

I believe that you and I are both are truly blessed.

I BELIEVE IN MIRACLES.

WHAT DO
YOU BELIEVE?

_____

_____

_____

_____

_____

_____

_____

_____

_____

_____

_____

_____

_____

ABOUT THE AUTHOR

WENDI BLUM is known as the Woman on a Health & Wellness Mission. An international speaker, business and life coach, and author, Wendi is dedicated to spreading words of inspiration and positivity everywhere she goes. She leads seminars, local and international retreats, and gives talks on dozens of subjects related to living your best life.

Wendi is available for lectures and programs worldwide. To obtain more information, please visit www.wendiblumpresents.com.

MANY BLESSINGS
TO YOU...